# Life Cycle of a

# Kangaroo

## Angela Royston

Heinemann
**LIBRARY**

First published in Great Britain by Heinemann Library
Halley Court, Jordan Hill, Oxford OX2 8EJ
a division of Reed Educational and Professional Publishing Ltd

Heinemann is a registered trademark of Reed Educational and Professional Publishing Limited.

Oxford   Florence   Prague   Madrid   Athens   Melbourne
Auckland   Kuala Lumpur   Singapore   Tokyo   Ibadan
Nairobi   Kampala   Johannesburg   Gaborone   Portsmouth NH
Chicago   Mexico City   São Paulo

Designed by Celia Floyd
Illustrations by Alan Fraser
Printed In Hong Kong by South China Printing Co. (1988) Ltd.

02 01 00 99
10 9 8 7 6 5 4 3 2 1

ISBN 0 431 08373 8
This title is also available in a hardback edition (ISBN 0431 08364 9)

**British Library Cataloguing in Publication Data**

Royston, Angela
   Life cycle of a kangaroo
   1.Kangaroos - Juvenile literature
   I.Title  II.Kangaroo
   599.2'22

**Acknowledgements**
The Publisher would like to thank the following for permission to reproduce photographs:
Bruce Coleman Ltd/CB & DW Frith p4; Bruce Coleman Ltd/D & J Bartlett p24; Bruce Coleman Ltd/Hans Reinhard p13; Bruce Coleman Ltd/John Canalosi p5, 10; Nature Focus/A Young p6; NHPA/A N T p15; NHPA/Dave Watts p20, 21; NHPA/Karl Switak p9; NHPA/Ken Griffiths pp18, 26/27; NHPA/Norbert Wu p25; OSF/Alan Root p7; OSF/David B Fleetham p17; OSF/Kathie Atkinson pp11, 16; OSF/Peter O'Toole p12; OSF/Stanley Breeden p22; OSF/Tom McHugh p19; Survival Anglia/D & J Bartlett p8, 14, 23.

Cover photograph: Art Wolfe/Tony Stone Images

# Contents

# Meet the kangaroos

There are 50 different kinds of kangaroo. One kind lives up in the trees. Another kind is as small as a rat. They are all found in Australia.

Newborn

5 months

7 months

The kangaroo in this book is a Grey kangaroo.

Every kangaroo spends the first few months of its life in its mother's **pouch**.

10–18 months

2 years

4 years

# Newborn

A baby kangaroo is called a **joey**.
Just before the joey is born, its
mother licks the inside of her **pouch**
to make it ready for the joey.

Newborn

5 months

7 months

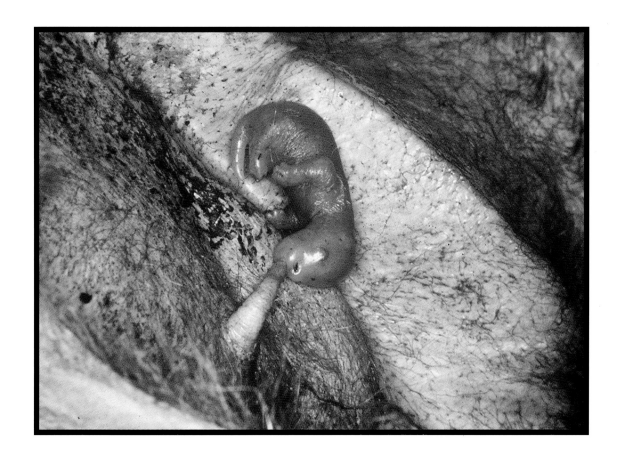

The newborn joey is tiny. It crawls through its mother's fur and into her pouch. There it finds a **teat** and holds on fast with its mouth.

10–18 months

2 years

4 years

# 5–6 months

The **joey** drinks milk from his mother and grows bigger. Sometimes he pops his head out of the **pouch** and looks around.

Newborn

5 months

7 months

The joey is safe inside the pouch. When his mother feeds, he nibbles some grass. But one day his mother tips him out of the pouch!

# 6–8 months

At first the **joey** is scared, but he is soon bouncing around. He loves to **box** and play with his mother.

Newborn

5 months

7 months

When he is thirsty, he just dips his head into her **pouch** for a drink of milk. When he is tired, he climbs back in.

10–18 months

2 years

4 years

# 8 months

While the **joey** plays, his mother looks out for danger. This eagle may be looking for a meal. It may attack the joey.

Newborn

5 months

7 months

His mother
calls to him
and the joey
dives head-
first into her
**pouch**. He is
safe now! He
turns around
inside the
pouch.

10–18 months

2 years

4 years

# 10–18 months

**14**

The **joey** is too big to get into the **pouch** now. He plays with the other joeys, but he still drinks his mother's milk.

Newborn

5 months

7 months

The joey likes to stay quite close to his mother. When she bounds away, he hurries after her!

10–18 months

2 years

4 years

# 18 months–2 years

The kangaroos and **joeys** stay together in a big group. They feed on grass and leaves.

Newborn

5 months

7 months

They feed early in the morning or late at night. During the heat of the day, they rest in the shade of the trees.

10–18 months

2 years

4 years

# 2–3 years

The young kangaroo leaves his mother. He is big enough to look after himself now. He bounds over the grass on his strong back legs.

Newborn

5 months

7 months

His long tail helps him to balance
as he flies through the air. He joins
a group of other young males.

# 4 years

One evening the young kangaroo notices a female. He wants to **mate** with her, but so does another male. The two males begin to fight.

Newborn

5 months

7 months

They grab each other with their front legs. Then the young kangaroo leans back on his tail and kicks with both feet.

10–18 months

2 years

4 years

# 4 years

The female watches as the young male wins the fight. He nuzzles her and clucks gently until she is ready to **mate**.

Newborn

5 months

7 months

Forty days after mating, a new joey will be born. It grows inside the female's pouch.

10–18 months

2 years

4 years

# Living in the bush

**Dingoes** are the kangaroos'
enemy. A **pack** of dingoes can
surround a kangaroo and
attack it.

Newborn

5 months

7 months

The kangaroos have smelt the dingo! They bound away, thumping the ground with their back legs as they go.

10–18 months

2 years

4 years

# Living in the bush

The **dingo** isn't the kangaroo's only enemy. If a kangaroo wanders onto farmland, the farmer may shoot him.

But if the kangaroo stays in the **bush**, he may live for 15 years, grazing among the trees with the other kangaroos.

# Life cycle

## Newborn joey

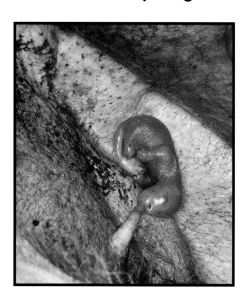

## 5 months

## 7 months

## 10 months

## 2 years

## 4 years

# Fact file

A newborn **joey** is 2.5 centimetres long, not even as long as your little finger.

A fully grown male Grey kangaroo is as tall as a man. Some Red kangaroos grow even taller.

A kangaroo can jump 13.5 metres. In one bound it could jump over three cars parked end to end.

A kangaroo can move as fast as a car (up to 64 kilometres per hour) to escape from danger.

# Glossary

**box**   playful fighting

**bush**   the Australian word for open countryside

**dingo**   a kind of wild dog found in Australia

**joey**   a young kangaroo from the time it is born until it is old enough to look after itself

**mate**   to come together (a female and a male) to produce young

**pouch**   a pocket of skin across a female kangaroo's stomach

**teat**   a place from where a baby can drink milk from its mother

# Index